WHAT PROTECTS US DURING NATURAL DISASTERS?

LISA OWINGS

LERNER PUBLICATIONS • MINNEAPOLIS

Content consultant: Ayman Mosallam, American Society of Civil Engineers Fellow and Professor of Civil and Environmental Engineering, The Henry Samueli School of Engineering, University of California–Irvine

Lerner Publications Company
A division of Lerner Publishing Group, Inc.
241 First Avenue North
Minneapolis, MN 55401 USA

For reading levels and more information, look up this title at www.lernerbooks.com.

Main body text set in Caecilia Com 55 Regular 11/16
Typeface provided by Linotype AG.

Library of Congress Cataloging-in-Publication Data

Owings, Lisa, author.
    What protects us during natural disasters? / Lisa Owings.
        pages   cm. — (Engineering keeps us safe)
    Audience: Ages 9–12.
    Audience: Grades 4 to 6.
        Includes bibliographical references and index.
        ISBN 978-1-4677-7914-2 (lb : alk. paper) — ISBN 978-1-4677-8649-2 (eb pdf)
        1. Natural disasters—Safety measures—Juvenile literature. 2. Natural disasters—Prevention—Juvenile literature. 3. Natural disaster warning systems—Juvenile literature. 4. Structural engineering—Juvenile literature.
    I. Title.
    GB5019.O95 2016
    363.34—dc23   2014046774

Manufactured in the United States of America
1 – VP – 7/15/15

CONTENTS

DESIGNING FOR DISASTER

When a natural disaster strikes, it's all over the news.
Cameras pan across towns flattened by tornadoes.
Newspapers detail damage from earthquakes and floods.
Warnings and pleas for help stream from the television. News
sources know people are fascinated by natural disasters.
Covering them means more viewers, readers, and money. And
with today's technology, these stories can be shared with the
rest of the world in seconds. That can make it seem as if the
next big disaster is always just around the corner.

The good news is major disasters don't happen often. And
when they do, technology and smart design help us predict
them and protect ourselves. You have less than a 1 in 3,000
chance of dying in any natural disaster. In fact, you're much
more likely to die simply from falling down. And the odds of
dying in a natural disaster continue to go down. After each
disaster, we learn from our mistakes. Engineers work to
improve the technologies and structures that protect us during
these events. Their designs keep us safe, even if we can't
control nature.

TWISTER!

News outlets run stories about natural disasters because they know such stories will catch the public's attention.

Tornado tore up houses on 68th St. in Brooklyn.

Tornado hits Bay Ridge; rains swamp city

COMPLETE COVERAGE ON PAGES 2-8

BUILDINGS OF GLASS

As storms go, hurricanes and tornadoes are often the biggest. These funnel-shaped storms rotate like spinning tops. Hurricanes form over warm oceans. Whirling winds and rain from these giant storms can destroy coastal cities. Tornadoes form over land. They are smaller but more violent. Their winds can reach speeds of more than 300 miles (480 kilometers) per hour. Luckily, weather experts are good at predicting these storms. They use satellites and radar to track them. Weather experts try to warn people when the storms are likely to hit. But it's hard to hide from such powerful winds.

Engineers design homes and other buildings to stand up to strong winds. Windstorms carry debris that can easily break traditional glass windows and doors. Modern builders use glass that is much harder to break. Impact glass is made by sandwiching a layer of plastic between two pieces of glass. Then the whole thing is heated up and melted together. The plastic makes the glass less likely to shatter. Even if the glass breaks, the plastic holds the shards, or pieces, in place. Testers simulate objects hitting the glass and strong winds blowing against it to make sure it won't break in a storm.

Tornadoes are destructive windstorms, but by using proper building materials and preparing, people can often prevent some damage.

Storm shutters are easy and quick to close, so they can be used at a moment's notice.

Storm shutters are another way to keep glass from breaking. The metal or plastic shutters can be slid over windows before a storm hits. Locks keep the shutters from blowing open. For tall buildings, engineers design large shutters and screens that roll out at the touch of a button. Motors move the shutters over the glass and lock them. When no storms are in sight, the shutters can be rolled up again.

BUILT FOR WIND

Hurricanes and tornadoes don't just blow out windows. They can tear apart whole buildings, especially those made of wood. Roofs are often the weakest part of a structure. Strong winds might lift the roof off a wooden house, which can cause walls to collapse. Hurricane clips are one solution. Builders install metal plates that fasten roofs to the tops of walls and roof beams. Similar plates strengthen joints between floors. Special bolts are used to anchor the bottoms of walls to the building's foundation. These bolts are usually set in wet concrete in the foundation. When the concrete dries, the bolts hold firm. Buildings with hurricane clips and anchor bolts are much harder to topple.

Engineers also know the shape of a building can prevent wind damage. Round or dome-shaped buildings allow wind to flow smoothly around instead of pushing roughly against walls and roofs. And less material is needed to build a round shape. So less of a round building's surface is exposed to wind. No wonder circular homes have become popular in hurricane zones. Each circular home has a strong column in the center. Floor and roof beams connect to this central support like spokes on a wheel. Spokes support your bicycle wheels and keep the wheels from crumpling. Similarly, the beams keep walls and roofs from blowing off or caving in.

Dome-shaped homes are safer in hurricanes than are homes with flat sides. Their shape allows the wind to move around them instead of against them.

WIND MACHINES

Engineers don't have to wait for a storm to test their designs. The University of Florida has a large hurricane simulator. Its eight fans blow high winds at homes and buildings. Water jets show the effects of rain. The Wall of Wind *(right)* at Florida International University has twelve fans. The indoor hurricane conditions it creates are used to test models of homes.

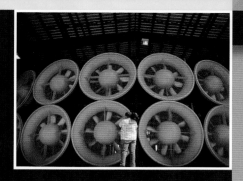

SAFE HAVENS

In the most severe storms, safe rooms and storm shelters offer maximum protection. These structures are as stormproof as it gets. Safe rooms are used in homes and other buildings to protect small groups of people. In the United States, the Federal Emergency Management Agency (FEMA) sets rules for these rooms. They must be made of reinforced concrete or plywood layered with strong steel. These materials keep flying objects from piercing walls or ceilings. The doors are often designed to open inward in case debris piles up outside. Safe rooms can be built aboveground or belowground. As long as they are attached to a strong foundation, they will live up to their name.

Public storm shelters have to meet the same standards as safe rooms but on a larger scale. The most effective shelters are those built underground. Dome shelters are some of the

HOW SAFE ARE SAFE ROOMS?

According to FEMA, safe rooms must be able to stand up to winds of 250 miles (400 km) per hour. More important, they should shield against heavy objects—even cars—falling or flying. In a common test, a machine fires heavy wooden boards at a safe room's weakest spots at 100 miles (160 km) per hour. If the room gets dents more than 3 inches (8 centimeters) deep, it would be unsafe during a tornado. So far, nearly everyone who has taken shelter in a safe room that follows FEMA's rules has survived strongest and most wind resistant. They can also cover large areas easily. One dome could enclose an entire football field and thousands of fans! The domes are formed inside giant balloons. Workers line the balloon with foam and steel to help it keep its shape. Then they spray the inside with a thick layer of concrete. When the concrete dries, the dome can stand up to the fiercest storms without any supports inside. So the space under the dome can stay completely open. Dome shelters can hold large crowds and double as gyms or community centers.

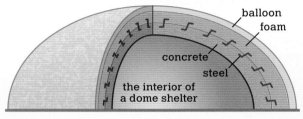

LAYERS OF A DOME SHELTER

balloon
foam
concrete
steel
the interior of
a dome shelter

Storm shelters belowground are sturdy and safe against the strongest winds.

FROM THE BOTTOM UP

Earthquakes pose a threat to many parts of the world. Most earthquakes happen along faults, where pieces of Earth's crust rub together. Suddenly the ground begins shaking violently. Sometimes the earth breaks apart. If buildings aren't designed well, they can come tumbling down. It's the job of engineers to design buildings so lives are saved during earthquakes.

It's a challenge to keep the base of a building stable during earthquakes. Earth's movements shift buildings from side to side. But engineers have designed a slick solution. Base isolation lets buildings move separately from the ground beneath them. There are several types of base isolation. Some of the common ones use rubber pads around metal cores. Builders space layers of pads evenly between the bottom of a building and its foundation. A metal core is placed inside each set of pads. The metal keeps the pads from getting crushed under the weight of the building. But the softer rubber can still squish from side to side. When an earthquake hits, the pads move with the ground. The building stays steady.

BASE-ISOLATED BUILDING

base isolation

stiffening plates

lead center

before an earthquake

rubber layers

during an earthquake

building foundation

earthquake waves

ground movement

Other types of base isolation use metal plates. Top plates are attached to the building. Bottom plates are fastened to the ground. Between each set of plates is a round ball that moves on a slick, curved surface. This lets the plates slide freely. The building can move side to side or up and down, opposite the motion of the ground.

Earthquakes can severely damage buildings that aren't built with base isolation.

SHAKE TABLE TESTING

Engineers use shake tables to test their earthquake designs. Most tables test only small models. But the world's largest indoor shake table can test full-size structures. Built in Japan, this table moves several feet in all directions. It can simulate the movements of a powerful earthquake. In 2009, it was used to test a seven-story building.

BAD VIBRATIONS

Not all buildings, especially older buildings, are lucky enough to have base isolation. Shear walls are more common and less high tech. These walls are stiff and strong enough to reduce sideways motion. Most building frames are made up of columns and horizontal beams. They look like a bunch of rectangles. When an earthquake strikes, the ground moves sideways. The bottom of the frame moves with the ground while the top tries to stay put. The right angles of the rectangles move sideways and turn into slanted angles. When shear walls are attached to the frame, the extra support stops the rectangles from squishing. Shear walls are usually made of plywood panels. But in multistory buildings, they can be made of steel, concrete, or other materials. Shear walls are used on the insides and outsides of structures.

Dampers can also be built into building frames. Dampers help absorb some of the energy from earthquakes. Fluid dampers are one kind of energy absorber. They slow down the building's movements using liquid. These dampers are often installed in a building's cross braces. On one end of each damper is a cylinder filled with liquid. On the other end is a plunger that moves through the cylinder. When the building moves, the plunger is pushed or pulled through the liquid. Think about how your movements slow down in water. When fluid dampers are used, it's like the whole building is moving through water.

TUNED MASS DAMPERS

Some high-rise buildings use tuned mass dampers. These heavy weights are hung inside the top floors. They move on cables or springs. During an earthquake, the top of a skyscraper sways back and forth. A mass damper moves in the opposite direction. This helps keep the building stable. A building in Taipei, Taiwan, holds the largest mass damper in the world. It weighs 730 tons (662 metric tons)!

NEW IDEAS

Engineers are always coming up with new ideas to protect against earthquake damage. One design lets a building rock freely during a quake. Afterward, the building rights itself again. How does it work? Columns supporting the building are placed in steel "shoes." Within the shoes, the columns can rock and even lift off the ground. The shoes also hold steel plates that absorb some of the energy from the rocking. These plates can be replaced after each earthquake. Steel cables run up the sides of the building. They keep it from swaying out of control. The cables work like strong rubber bands. They stretch with the building's movements. Then, when the quake is over, they return to their original shape. In doing so, they pull the building back into position.

Have you ever heard of a floating home? Japanese engineers are exploring this idea. Sensors in the foundation feel the beginning of an earthquake. Within seconds, a cushion between the home and its foundation fills with air. It lifts the home a short distance off the ground. Like base isolation, this allows the earth to move while the home stays still. When the earthquake stops, the home gently sinks back to the ground.

Equally amazing are materials that can repair themselves. Some materials do this naturally. Others can do it with a little extra help. Engineers are studying ways to help metal, concrete, and other building materials heal minor cracks.

Buildings' smaller cracks that are caused by earthquakes may one day be able to fix themselves with the use of "smart" materials.

One way is to add tiny capsules filled with protective liquid substances, such as glue. When the building is subjected to large forces, the material cracks, and the capsules break open. The protective substance fills in the cracks and then hardens so the material stays strong. Such "smart" materials could reduce repairs needed after an earthquake.

FIRST LINES OF DEFENSE

Wildfires burn through dry forests or prairies. Small mistakes can trigger building fires that spread quickly. But unlike some other disasters, we can often stop fires from starting or spreading.

In many countries, flame retardants are used to prevent fires. These chemicals are often added to wires, wood, and paint. They are also applied to walls, ceilings, and roofs in many buildings. During a fire, the chemicals react in a few ways. Some cool off the burning surface, slowing or stopping the fire. Others release water vapor or other gases that take the place of oxygen in the room. Without enough oxygen to fuel it, the fire goes out. Flame retardants can also form barriers between fire and flammable material.

If a fire does start, smoke detectors issue a warning. Some work by sensing changes in light. A beam of light shines

PREVENTING BUILDING COLLAPSE

Engineers must account for the possibility of a fire in their building design. For multistory steel buildings, load-bearing parts must be protected from fire so the building will not collapse. There are two common types of protection. The first includes gypsum boards and mineral fiberboard with resin. These are commonly attached to steel or wood framing to protect against fire damage. The second type of protection is applied to the structural parts like paint. These paints or coatings can resist heat up to 482°F (250°C).

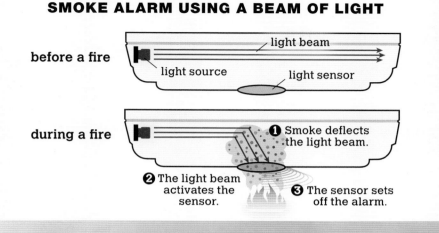

SMOKE ALARM USING A BEAM OF LIGHT

before a fire

light beam

light source

light sensor

during a fire

❶ Smoke deflects the light beam.

❷ The light beam activates the sensor.

❸ The sensor sets off the alarm.

inside the detector. If smoke gets in, the light bounces off the smoke. This triggers the alarm to sound. Other detectors use an electric current. It's like plugging something into an outlet. When smoke gets in, it breaks the current, just like pulling the plug. Then the alarm sounds.

Once people hear the fire alarm and exit the building, the fire still needs to be stopped. Fire extinguishers are designed to put out small fires. Simple ones hold water that can be sprayed on the fire. Others spray foams or powders that act like a blanket, smothering the fire. A fire extinguisher can spray several feet so users can stand at a safe distance. Pins or seals keep extinguishers from going off accidentally.

Wildfires can burn thousands of acres of land. To try to contain them, helicopters may fly overhead and drop fire retardants around the wildfire.

AUTOMATIC FIRE CONTROL

Sprinkler systems are even better than extinguishers at stopping fires. They don't require anyone to be there to use them. Engineers have designed these tools to work automatically. Homes and other buildings with these systems have pipes in their ceilings or walls. The pipes run to sprinkler heads that point down from the ceiling. Often the pipes are filled with water and ready to go. But the sprinklers are designed not to go off unless they really need to.

Each sprinkler head becomes active only when it senses the heat from a fire. The hole where the water sprays out is closed in one of two ways. Some sprinklers use a type of metal that melts at fiery temperatures. Others use a small glass bulb filled with liquid. The liquid expands at high temperatures and breaks the glass. When the metal melts or the glass breaks, the sprinkler head opens to spray water over the fire. Most often, only one or two sprinklers go off. This keeps water damage down. But sprinklers can be set to flood the area to try to stop the fire immediately. However, water damages electrical equipment and won't put out grease fires. In these and other special cases, sprinklers spray foams or other chemicals instead.

When a sprinkler head senses heat from a fire, it will spray either water or foam to extinguish the fire.

THIN AIR

Some buildings have an even more advanced way to prevent or fight fires. They have sealed rooms where oxygen levels are kept too low for fires to start. Sensors in the room keep track of oxygen levels. The system constantly adjusts the oxygen levels so they are high enough for people to breathe but low enough to prevent a fire. If a fire does break out, some systems can bring oxygen levels down further to smother it.

HARNESSING THE FLOOD

All living things need water to survive. But during floods and tsunamis (giant ocean waves), water can also destroy homes and other buildings. Some floods happen with rains or snowmelts each year and are easy to predict. Others come after surprise storms. Tsunamis usually form during undersea earthquakes or other disasters. Tsunamis travel quickly, hit hard, and can rise more than 100 feet (30 meters) once they hit the coast. People who live near water do as much as they can to prevent and prepare for these disasters.

Where rivers flood regularly, engineers design dams to hold back their waters. Concrete and other strong materials form a tall, heavy wall across a river. Water collects behind the dam. Instead of flooding the land, the water is stored in a large reservoir. The water in the reservoir can then be released slowly or put to use.

Dams designed for floods need a way to let out excess water. Otherwise, the water can flow over or break the dam. Spillways solve this problem. These are openings near the top of the dam with chutes leading down the

After they've passed, tsunamis leave lasting and widespread flood damage (above).

dry side. Most of the time, water does not reach the spillways. But during floods, small amounts of water flow through them and out the other side of the dam. This protects the dam and keeps large amounts of water from flooding the river.

Floodwater stored behind dams can be very useful. The water is drawn down through pipes. It can then be used for drinking or to water crops. Some dams use the water for generating electric power. A pipe near the bottom of the dam draws in water. The water flowing down through the dam spins the blades of a turbine. This motion produces electricity. Floodwater can be used to power whole cities!

Some dams are built to hold back floodwater. They keep the water from flooding the land and either release the water over time or put it to use.

BUILDING BARRIERS

Several other types of barriers protect us from flood-prone waters. Some are always left in place. Floodwalls are often built using concrete and steel. The bottom of the wall is buried several inches below the ground. This helps keep the wall from being knocked over. Levees are typically made of mounded earth and clay. The clay is dense enough to keep water from leaking through. Plants atop the levee keep the soil from washing away.

Seawalls are built along coasts to keep tsunamis and other large waves from harming people and buildings. Most are made of concrete or stone. Curved seawalls force waves upward and back. This reduces the energy of the wave. A curved rim can also keep the wave from flowing over the wall. Many seawalls use piles of rough stone or concrete blocks. The loose, uneven surface absorbs and scatters the wave's energy.

Other barriers stay open most of the time, closing only during a flood. In the United Kingdom, the Thames Barrier protects London from flooding. A row of stainless steel gates stretches across the River Thames. When the gates are open, water and boats move freely over them. During a flood, motors between the gates rotate them upward. Together they form a solid steel wall.

The Thames Barrier in London is made of stainless steel gates that rotate to

Curved seawalls protect people and buildings from large waves.

RISING ABOVE AND FLOWING THROUGH

Many homes and other buildings in flood-prone areas are designed to sit above the floodwaters. They are built atop strong columns. If the area floods, water passes between the columns instead of crashing into walls. The columns need to be firmly attached to both the ground and the base of the structure so the water doesn't carry them away. Stainless steel plates are often used because water does not weaken them over time.

Engineers have also designed ways to let water flow through a building with minimal damage. Flood vents across the bottoms of buildings act like gates. They stay shut until water rises past the bottom of the vent. Latches on the vent are connected to floats. As water levels rise, the floats lift. They automatically open the vents. Water and debris can then flow freely through the building. By giving the water a place to go, engineers keep the flood from making its own path.

Some structures have living or storage spaces below flood levels. Many of these buildings have breakaway walls. The columns between the walls hold strong. But the walls are designed to collapse easily in a flood or a tsunami. This gives the water an easy path and keeps it from knocking down the whole building. And the supporting columns keep the main structure and the people inside it safe. Rooms with breakaway walls are often built of waterproof materials. This way, the rooms may not suffer much damage even after a flood or a tsunami has surged through them.

STAYING AFLOAT

Floating homes may be the next big thing in flood design. Architects in the United Kingdom built a home out of lightweight wood. It sits on a concrete structure designed to float. When a flood hits, the house rises within its foundation. It sits on the water's surface like a boat. Posts around the home keep it in place until the water levels go down.

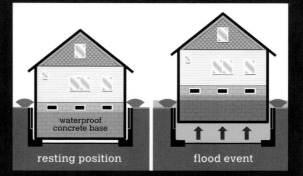

resting position

flood event

waterproof concrete base

Homes in flood-prone areas may be built on strong columns. Floodwater passes by the columns and beneath the home.

IMPROVED DESIGN AND STRUCTURES

It's good to be prepared for natural disasters. But we don't have to live in fear of them. Scientists are getting better at predicting these events and warning those affected ahead of time. And engineers study how natural disasters work and what damage they cause. They design buildings and other structures that save lives during hurricanes, tornadoes, earthquakes, fires, and floods. Not every design is perfect. But each unexpected disaster gives us a chance to test and improve the structures that protect us. Every day, engineers around the world are exploring new ways to meet Earth's fiercest challenges. So the next time you hear about a disaster in the news, rest assured that engineers' designs can keep you safe.

GLOSSARY

automatically: working without direct control by a person

capsule: a very small container filled with something

cross braces: diagonal elements within the frame that make an X

debris: pieces of something that has been destroyed

flammable: quick to catch fire and burn

foundation: the structure that supports a home or other building from underneath, often belowground

frame: the skeleton of a building, or the basic structure that supports it

reservoir: a human-made lake used to store water

resistant: not easily affected or harmed by something

simulate: to look, feel, or act like something

turbine: an engine powered by water or wind moving through its blades

SELECTED BIBLIOGRAPHY

Britt, Robert Roy. "The Odds of Dying." *Livescience.* January 6, 2005. http://www
.livescience.com/3780-odds-dying.html.

Diacu, Florin. *Megadisasters: The Science of Predicting the Next Catastrophe.*
Princeton, NJ: Princeton UP, 2010.

"Fire Prevention and Control." *Encyclopædia Britannica.* Accessed December 29,
2014. http://www.britannica.com/EBchecked/topic/207866/fire-prevention
-and-control.

"Taking Shelter from the Storm: Building a Safe Room for Your Home or Small
Business." FEMA. August 2008. Accessed November 11, 2014. https://www
.fema.gov/media-library/assets/documents/2009.

"The Thames Barrier." Gov.uk. July 30, 2014. https://www.gov.uk/the-thames
-barrier.

FURTHER INFORMATION

Disaster Master
http://www.ready.gov/kids/games/data/dm-english/index.html
Do you know what to do during natural disasters? Play this fun game to test your skills.

Earthquakes by Claire and Nisha
http://pbskids.org/dragonflytv/show/earthquakes.html
Watch this video to learn how Earth moves during earthquakes.

Know the Facts, Be Empowered!
http://www.ready.gov/kids/know-the-facts
Find out more about what causes natural disasters and how to protect yourself.

Kostigen, Thomas. *Extreme Weather: Surviving Tornadoes, Sandstorms, Hailstorms, Blizzards, Hurricanes, and More!* Washington, DC: National Geographic, 2014. Check out this book for ways to stay safe during even the most severe weather.

Lusted, Marcia Amidon. *Surviving Natural Disasters*. Minneapolis: Lerner Publications, 2014.
Not sure what you would do if a disaster struck? Read these true stories about real people who lived through natural disasters.

Royston, Angela. *Science vs. Natural Disasters*. New York: Gareth Stevens, 2013. Read more about the role science plays in protecting us from Earth's worst weather.

Tarshis, Lauren. *I Survived the Japanese Tsunami, 2011*. New York: Scholastic, 2013.
Follow the story of a boy who lived through the 2011 earthquake and tsunami in Japan.

Tornadoes
http://www.ready.gov/kids/know-the-facts/tornado
Be ready with the knowledge of what to do before, during, and after a tornado hits.

INDEX

PHOTO ACKNOWLEDGMENTS

The images in this book are used with the permission of: © JT images/ Moment/Getty Images, p. 1; AP Photo/David Mercer, p. 5 (inset); © New York Daily News/Getty Images, p. 5 (background); © Carsten Peter/National Geographic/Getty Images, p. 6; REUTERS/Dave Martin /Landov , p. 7; Paul Brou/ZUMAPRESS/Newscom, p. 9; © Joe Raedle/Getty Images, p. 9 (top); AP Photo/Charlie Riedel, p. 10; © Laura Westlund/Independent Picture Service, pp. 11 (top), 12, 27 (inset); © Larry Miller/Science Source, p. 11 (bottom); © Tayfun Coskun/Anadolu Agency/Getty Images, p. 13; Wikimedia Commons (CC BY-SA 3.0), p. 13 (inset); Mark E. Gibson/Ambient Images//Newscom, p. 15; © Sean Pavone/Alamy, p. 15 (inset); © Marc Hill/Alamy, p. 17; © FREDRIK SANDBERG/AFP/Getty Images, pp. 18-19; © Don Farrall/Photographer's Choice RF/Getty Images, p. 21; © Yoshinori Kuwahara/Moment/Getty Images, p. 22; © Guenter Fischer/Getty Images, p. 23; © Andrew Holt/Photographer's Choice/ Getty Images, p. 24; © Premium UIG/Universal Images Group/Getty Images, p. 25; © Fuse/Getty Images, p. 27; AP Photo/Sue Ogrocki, p. 28.

Front cover: © Oksanaphoto/Dreamstime.com.